ALSO BY CYNTHIA ZARIN

Poetry

The Swordfish Tooth

Fire Lyric

For Children

Rose and Sebastian

What Do You See When You Shut Your Eyes?

Wallace Hoskins, The Boy Who Grew Down

The Watercourse

THE
WATERCOURSE

Poems

CYNTHIA ZARIN

*To Colleen Allen Fortune,
with best regards
from
Cynthia Zarin*

March 2002

Alfred A. Knopf   New York   2002

THIS IS A BORZOI BOOK
PUBLISHED BY ALFRED A. KNOPF

www.randomhouse.com/knopf/poetry

Knopf, Borzoi Books, and the colophon are
registered trademarks of Random House, Inc.

Grateful acknowledgment is made to *The New Criterion*,
The Paris Review, *Western Humanities Review*, and *The Yale
Review*, where some of these poems appeared in slightly
different form. The following poems first appeared in *The New
Yorker:* "The Astronomical Hen," "Bruise," "Harriet," "The
May Apple," sections I and V of "Port Imperial"
(as "Hawk Watching" and "Angelus"), and "Primrose." "Primrose"
also appeared in the anthology *Poems for the New Century*
(New York Public Library/Aralia Press, 1996), and "Baby's Breath"
in *Of Leaf and Flower* (Persea Books, 2001).

Library of Congress Cataloging-in-Publication Data
Zarin, Cynthia.
The watercourse : poems / by Cynthia Zarin.
        p.   cm.
ISBN 0-375-41366-9
I. Title.
PS3576.A69 W38 2002
811'.54—dc21   2001038225

Manufactured in the United States of America
First Edition

To Harry and Kathleen Ford

CONTENTS

I

I

Spode Plate

A branch sprouting from its crook a chrysanthemum,
and below, new leaves, a grass snake, a pale line

in the glaze that between us, we can call a river.
Stars, smatterings of the old crowd—Andromeda, Orion,

the bear cub, and now, far off, you. How in heaven
did the plate get so dirty? I rinse it with soap

and water, I scrub like a child taught to have faith
in washing, then furiously, my back a question

mark, my hunch the crouch of a crone with an ear
to the ground, a doubter, but a cloud remains

over the flaring sun and the coiled serpent, smudging
the wry plain of stars. I didn't know this could happen.

I thought if you scrubbed, the stain would dissolve in
the water used to douse it, and the scene—the burning

tree with its too-heavy bright bloom, the black stars
on the charred hill, the ragged maiden—would again

be a place that had heard nothing, and seen less,
a landscape of mild temperance, the smooth porcelain

alive with the sheen of reflected moonlight, where Orion
could shoot the bear along the river, and miss, and miss.

Harriet

Why did I say what I did to Harriet?
She was my age: nine, I don't think ten—
a kind of taunting I'd not do again.
Not to Harriet, who for me still
limps up the hill, jacket torn, stained skirt rent.
Harriet who wasn't beautiful yet.
Monster is what the mirror said to me—
I opened my mouth and Harriet fled.
Now those words are breath, there's no sound
but the hissing wind in the wild trees,
and Harriet falling, as she didn't then.

Bruise

Black bruise an inch
below my knee; white bone, my
kneecap wrenched askew;

knee a blind eye, bruise
a shiner, the pair of them two
goggle-eyes, bridged by

a shiny, half-moon scar.
A battered aviatrix? She
flies above a dream island.

At three, I fell from
a knee-high curb. *Mind yourself,*
I hear the voices say,

when decades later,
in the bath, my knee, drowned
face, knucklehead, rises

above the water table,
volcano with its violet flame.
Bedpost? Doorjamb?

The hours last week
turned to glass? And if asked
to swear to it, say

what's to blame?
The mind trolls, reels back,
and begins, and begins

again to prove how if
I'd only done that one thing—
but there are so many.

The Astronomical Hen

Like hearts marked out but not yet colored in,
Each of her feathers has a black edge,
as if an India-ink mantilla stretched

from uncleaved neck to her fantail. The pen,
homemade, spilled some darkness now and then.
She doesn't lack for suitors. Poor rooster,

who pours his own loud heart out to her,
surely his begging does no more than force
her to peck out a crooked tattoo in the dirt

of the pen. Is she stumped, sad, anorexic?
It's perfectly clear she doesn't lay eggs.
Can it be she's simply in love with herself?

Her eye obsidian, eye of the world,
at night she watches the stars drop from shelf
to shelf, to minor études she unfurls

in her head. By day she hunts and re-pecks
the pinprick holes of her intricate sketch.
If she's done by dusk the first stars can rise.

Mrs. Donleavey

"There's Mrs. Donleavey," someone said,
and pointed to where she stood in her cloud
of nightgown, twenty yards up from where

five of us waited for the school bus to stop.
Her flood of gold hair was stained with damp.
Rosebuds grew from the gauze and marl

of her body. She hummed, and the long
braid of sound came down to us, a blind snake
in the garden, and though I held back I wanted

to leap and catch it, to grapple, to hoist
myself up into what I even then knew would be
the lap of grief. It was a cool morning

in early spring. Dew polished the dragon
leaves of the laurel, the blue hydrangea,
the boxwood whose dense green scales sprang

back at my touch, from my hand that blocked
her from view when the bus pulled away
with me at the window, and my palm left a smudge

that within days came to mark like a plume
of smoke her complete disappearance
from our street—or so I thought I'd heard,

under a rush of water and the radio—into
a past I believed was hers only, and that
seemed to me then sheer, inconsolable, new.

The Deanery Parrot

TO JAMES AND PAMELA MORTON

Stutterer, loiterer, his cage a Taj Mahal—
  springwater, millet, no
    effort spared; day a private
view of morning glories, a dish
  of savories; night a Liberty shawl

    thrown across his aviary. Yet
the parrot is unhappy in the heart
  of the house, jumping as his blood
    jumps, at his own harsh
sound. Nothing pleases him. Beset—

  no one else ever *stops* talking—
    he won't even repeat what's
said to him. Instead, he stumps up
    and down, plucking his belly feathers out;
      his underside's a mess of ticking.

How terrible to have him here! Even
  let loose, he remains—he has
    no call to be away. What can
be done short of doing him in? The bird
  psychiatrist has twice been

  paid, the veterinarian, poor
man, has come to stay. Captivity's
  a habit, they both say. What
    about aniseed? Cognac? Watercress?
No go. To him, apparently, more

9

is less—Doloroso on the skids
had a countenance cheerier
than his red gaze, which conveys
he's witnessed not only
The Fall, but ours, and is

appalled. (And our end? Parrots,
heaven help us, can outlive
their owners.) Since Tuesday
last, he's hopped on one leg, having
overheard—one can but

guess—a dinner guest from Delhi
describe a holy man, who, steeped
in the *asanas*, has spent twenty
years in Tree Pose, his left
foot inscribed on his right knee.

Holy moly, what a show-off—
the nightshade please!
But then the sun catches his feathers—
what's left of them—and
turns them to blue fire.

On Reading a Collected Letters

The rationing, the slugs on the lawn, the spirit
    lamp casting up the mute face of
    the charwoman's dead child, the elephantine
      car that made it through another

winter, the hoarfrost dotting the lawn. An utter
    frenzy of communication, of agendas
    surprisingly fulfilled in the glossy umber
      evenings with—downstairs—the wireless

going, each typed letter (for later, she typed
    them) a stitch in the seam every so
    often righted by an exclamation, a scrawled
      postscript, glad at the prospect of

a real visit. Tea and scones. The peanut butter
    it was impossible to get in Hampstead
    arriving in the post, kites the Folies-
      Bergère colors of tulips

on Tuesday over the downs, then rain—a torrent—
    on Whitsun which finished off
    the raspberries; all this welter
      of stamps and paper a dumb show

of feeling, the wood, now that it's so hard
    to get warm, chopped by the extraordinary
    Mr. Pillager, who is so faithful about
      lending a hand, whose wife

has a gold sewing scissor shaped like a crane
  with a garnet eye, which was given
  to her by her "previous employment."
    But this hand lent, given

to correspondence, to writing salutations
  and envoies, the light blue envelope
  the same color as the sky above
    Euston Station where she always

bought a same day return, the torn half
  marking the lost chapter of the story
  which is silent in these pages,
    measured out now in centimeters,

sausages and jam, a deliberate feigned ignorance
  that some things are being done
  for the last time, but for a few italicizations—
    a snow goose, an illness—until

she herself is like a signature gone quill-thin
  but nevertheless possible to make out
  under a strong reading lamp, kept on
    past midnight by the thought

of her having just now gone out, as if
  for stamps and paper, carried—a deliverance—
  through those light-as-air
    just wide enough doors.

Eclogue

(TO AMY CLAMPITT)

"Our neighbor, a retired engineer, comes to clip
our hedge, the cardinals come in pairs, but sometimes
singly—their red is black against the lap of green."
Lenox in August, the high blood brick front of the library
peeling white. *I wish, I wish*—the helicopter seeds
of the plane trees spin but do not touch your door.
I wish—onstage the dollmaker's daughter springs
to life, the Nutcracker Prince rides the swan boat.
You do not stir. Tableau vivant, you sail out
on your white bed. We went from you to Wharton's
Mount. Only Rose, in her third summer, braved
the No Admittance sign. "Hullo," she said, "Papa's
calling me." Her exit is her entrance, the words
summer afternoon skittering like hoops down the hill.

Envoy

(TO JOSEPH BRODSKY)

Every premonition has its points. The *Coronation*
Mass turns on by itself; one candle sheds
more light than another; black thread unspools
and winds around a leg. Primroses for the dead:
when the Mayor called to offer you a place
on San Michele, the opera house went up in flames.
Fenice? True, every phoenix needs its ash, but
nothing, Joseph, is more surprising than surprise.
Radiant cruciform, lit harbor of cherry trees, sky
marbled with dusk, the children a flock of anemones,
of finches—heedless as Actaeon I return
to the garden and see you, heart in my mouth,
in your ninth life, searching the flagstones,
calling *Kitty, Kitty,* from the top of the stairs.

The Zoo in Winter

In the one warm day between two spheres
of cold—a day just warm enough to breathe—
we took the bus to see the zoo in winter.
Every branch and leaf was furred with ice.
At the sea lion pond, spray had sifted
sugar swirls around the rim (we couldn't see
through the glass for the white), but once
or twice a face peered out, a glimpse through lace
at a window. In the penguin house
the penguins never for moment stopped diving
and drying their piano-key wings in the cold.
A man cleaned the rocks with a huge mop—
an octopus that sat on top of its pole
like a fright wig. No one else came in.
Outside we were joined by a whole family
of children, each one a half-step smaller
than another, like notes on a xylophone.
There was a baby in a stroller. The polar
bear cub played with a ball and a block,
just like a real baby. We worried when
he came too close to the edge, batting his ball
with his sharp claws, and using the block
as a stepping-stone. Most of the water
was frozen over. His mother was sleeping.
The children, all six of them, wanted only
to climb the slippery, icy steps, to hide
themselves from the bear. *Watch out,*
      their mother said, *Hold on.*

The bear went on playing with his ball.
In a tank beside him, two harbor seals

swam swift as muskrats back and forth
under the green water, which by splashing
continuously over the barricade had left
a tiny seal of ice on the pavement
—snout, tail, shiny tilted head—as if
even it couldn't resist making something
    out of the cold.

Santuario de Chimayó

(New Mexico)

We thought the church would be bigger
but really it was no bigger than a one-room
schoolhouse. Inside there were pictures
  everywhere, painted on the walls,
  the ceiling, even on the awkward
  homely pews which had been brought
    at great expense from

  Española. The walls seemed to
breathe, or maybe it was that we were all of us
  inside a body, breathing in
    together. It was just as I'd
    imagined it might be to enter
    a retablo. I have one
    now on my bookshelf,

  a hat seller, hawking twenty
black-and-fawn hats, and often I go over them
  very closely, to discover
    the telling detail—a tipped brim,
    a band—to determine which I should
    choose for the day. But really
    the hats are attached

    to the rafters, and would just fit
my index finger. In niches along the walls
  at Chimayó, the saints, even
    those whose faces are ill drawn or
    whose postures are lackadaisical,
    are clearly scholars, each one
    kept long after to

learn the complicated verses
of suffering which at any moment they will
be called upon to repeat. Of
the assembled, San Rafael
is the most attentive, his black eyes
astonished. Is he simply
grateful for being

able to see? His gauchos are
red as a turkey wattle, and one of his wings
is dented—I like to think it
was knocked awry in his travels—
but in any case his wings, drawn here,
are more like the staunch colorful flags
or starched banners of

a country whose stamps show views
of mangoes and palms, where every breath of air is
remarked, where the fragile peeling
houses kneel on their legs like
spoonbills and are flooded each spring by
the exhaled water of flush
estuaries. But

there's only the one river in
the place he comes from. The fish he holds is just now
about to turn into a loaf
of bread, bread that by its nature
must be continually replaced
in the mouths of the hungry.
In Chimayó, at

the spot that became sanctified,
Don Bernando Abyeta, moved by a vision,

touched his tongue to the earth and was
cured of what books only describe
as "his illness." Behind the nave, in
a room where had there been one
a younger priest might

have read and slept, the place he marked
in the floor never deepens, though for almost two
hundred years the dirt has been licked
and tasted. In the face of such clear
evidence hardly anyone
who comes resists leaving word,
for taped or pinned up

on the walls like white butterflies
are handwritten requests for help. Near the door
hang discarded crutches: big, picked-
clean wing bones, strong as anyone,
man or angel, might wish for. Why is it
impossible for me to
leave the notes unread,

as if here and only here was
an answer? We left the chapel without tasting
the dirt or writing a message.
Outside our breath froze in the thin
cold air of the sharp mountains, which
had three times seen the cross dug
up at Chimayó,

and three times seen it return there
of its own accord. It was as in a picture
already painted, one which had
made us think of driving up to

hairpin roads above the valley where branches
snag like fishlines on the brushed
surface of the

river, so that we might look for
the church; a scene by a painter whose canvases
are the size of an eyelid, who
told us, "I have lived here now for
years, but I've never entered the church.
I don't need to, I can
imagine it."

Winter Elegy

Mouth full of weeds
  in a month of no
    rain. What careless

god was it that let
  your humid water
    rise? Now the beach

is cold, the pond
  frozen over. Nausicaa
    in her winter

furs steps toward
  your salt-streaked
    garrulity of leaves.

Skating in Harlem, Christmas Day

TO MARY JO SALTER

Beyond the ice-bound stones and bucking trees,
past bewildered Mary, the Meer in snow,
two skating rinks and two black crooked paths

are a battered pair of reading glasses
scratched by the skater's multiplying math.
Beset, I play this game of tic-tac-toe.

Divide, subtract. Who can tell if love surpasses?
Two noughts we've learned make one astonished O—
a hectic night of goats and compasses.

Folly tells the truth by what it's not—
one X equals a fall I'd not forgo.
Are ice and fire the integers we've got?

Skating backwards tells another story—
the risky star above the freezing town,
a way to walk on water and not drown.

You I See

You I see everywhere, you I see nowhere,
the less I seek to err, the less I'm right,
I see a shadow when there's no one there.

Bereft at dusk, I move from chair to chair.
Bleak heart, I try, but I can't put you right.
I see you everywhere, I see you nowhere.

Stumbling, stammering, I swallow air,
loudly disputing what is wrong or right,
I speak to shadows when nobody's there,

speeches that can do nothing to repair
those hours, that being over, can't come right
when nowhere is a place called everywhere,

of winding spiral stairs, a double pair
that never meet though I turn left and right.
I hear your shadow step, but you're not there.

I gave you my heart. Life isn't fair.
It's true, I knew: to you I had no right.
Heedless, I divined signs from anywhere

—a sword, a one-eyed cat, a happy pair—
that one day I would sleep, and think, and write.
Amused, you'd answer from the shadows there.

Primrose

All winter you kept yourself to yourself,
straitened, dumb, in the illegal fire escape
flower box: calyx, stem, sap, bud,

all at once and for all tucked in, spirit-flower
posthumously transferred from a florist's tub.
July, November, the strongbox snow discarded, your

ocelot's face marries the sun to itself, an orphan
Persephone, pulling herself hand over hand
from fire to fire, spring's last ember

the first conflagration of the earth returned,
the Primus stove lit, then out, then lit again
is her burning crown under the blue smoke of the trees.

The May Apple

Or mandrake. By the brook
I bent and parted the leaves.
Clefts. Veins. Smell

of musk, of mud. Tongue
slide of sap propelled,
shaking under the green.

Stung Io, her sentries
pale udder behind a bower—
day moon a white brow,

a chin sheer in water.
I wanted to put my face
to it, to its sheen

more animal than flower.

Fury

I saw Fury on the stair,
Beak in my heart,
But no one's there.
I saw Fury rattle a chair.
Crack in the mirror,
Cart drags the mare—
How does love stop?
How does it start?

I saw Fury all in satin.
"How can he love her?"
Asked the black wren.
"Sky fell down," said Mrs. Hen.
Where the crow flies
Is where it gets eaten—
Judge came back in
With a hung jury.

Black is the ribbon
On her nightgown.
Green the hangman
Who took her to town.
The table's set with fire,
Tears fill the tap—
Miracles happen
But not behind your back.

If I had a penny
Or a hundred or two,
I'd sail the world
Straight back to you.

The serpent eats a sparrow,
The wolf lies down—
Fury carries on
With a wheelbarrow.

Love blinks an eyelid,
Nothing is for sure.
Bang goes the hammer,
Echoes out the door.
Fury's whistling
The dead dark bright—
Hid star I wish
Upon the night.

Rotogravure

There was another life we knew each other
We were poor and hungry we lived in a palace
Cats supped in our place aloft we ate air
Trees were our nursemaids the moss sang to us
The door was heavy the reed gate was smashed
We drove through smoke we rode in carriages
We were far from the shore the ocean was near
The sky was jute the wet earth gray ash
We spoke in English in Russian we argued
The moon wore a mask the sun mirrored its moods
In the desert the thirsty went down to the water
Hummingbirds swarmed lions roared in quarries
Silence is an envelope noise is paper
This is a story poems come after stories

II

Port Imperial

Light as a toy, heading north or south,
the Port Imperial ferry goes forth,

its deck bright white as a wedding cake.
Never, never can it stray,

its channel is its right-of-way.
The river too is frosted white.

Your lips are moths in my snarled hair.
Struck dumb I want the tide to stay

deaf to any reprimand,
for the night to brim, alluvial,

for the clock at Port Imperial
to take its face out of its hands.

II

How long six days are, end to end;
the hours flag as they begin.
Time's map tells a detailed lie—
an index finger keeping us apart.
No rest in six, no stop to start;
just six—no foot—is always rent.
Not pleased, I'd halve it once again
and so split by expedient
of fractions we'd be skin to skin.
Then inch by inch, I'd chart the sky's
marked firmament from ear to shin,
until the sun and moon went round,
and your light heart, by sextant, found.

III

So as the hawk flies over the ridge's beak,
you sail over me, under me, wing, shoulder,
jib, sheet, breath material as air, bird shadow
the sky's quick fingerprint, as if the god
of wind had just begun to sing, after a long silence,
a mute wandering, and put his hands just there,
and there, to keep his balance. His hands

are the hawk's black wings, and the bereft
stars that in a dream now fall on those green
hills, absolved, recalled, are the river's upper
reaches talking back, about a summer's day,
a burlap boat that didn't sink. Your hands linked
are those great wings—I fall upwards as I drink—
my head a nest of feathers on your back.

IV

A lifetime spent unraveling leads to knots.
My hands are tied, untied; untidiness reigns.
I try to twist new yarn from what I've got,
the stubborn spindle jams and will not give.
Insomniac, I recount threads to sleep,
and frantic in my haste to stockpile skeins
weave gold from shorn Rapunzel's plait
and doing so lose track, forfeit the game.
Dear heart, my shoe is lost. I have no name.

V

One opens the book at random, opens the day,
reads the old architecture whose face runs
like a dog along the window while the sun plays
catch with itself, bounding from Sunday

to Sunday, speechless with desire.
What more could there be than this?
The beams of the cottage, the sheltering
bones of your hips, the great abbey

of the afternoon that fills, as we watch, with sound
and the voices trail back to you from the apse,
the nave, from the shell-shaped hollow
at the base of your throat that even as it says

what it wants, even as it wills it, holds back,
and a great threshing noise saws the air
when the new beams are sawn all over again as
they must be continually, and knowing this

our very words, making and undoing, are torn,
the color of blood. For why are you here
before me after all this time, time which was
mine alone, but now, because we have brought

each other here, belongs to you? We talk
to each other as birds do under the eaves,
like the swallows who return, and each time
find everything changed, everything different.

In the early morning the ferry comes back,
paddling the eddies, and the river is green
as a lizard, quiet in the pale yellow light.
At noon the sun blackens the boat as it
goes out, the passengers waving, throwing
bread to the hurly-burly of gulls.

At night the river is tar, phosphorescent,
a Catherine wheel of spawn and honeysuckle
turning in the white wake of the motor,
and the ferry returns for what it meant
to take: a parrot, a valise, a lucky coin,
a map of the world, its colors blurred.

How could there be such a place
without our knowing it? The town,
so pretty, where air and water mix,
　　　where metal in the soil
turns the earth the color
　　　of roses? The locust trees by

the river are undressing,
shedding their leaves in the current.
Is the town man-made? If you put out
　　　your hand, the railing fits,
and below is the step
　　　where you listened as voices bloomed

in the dark. But here your hand's
the point of departure. Open
your fist. There's the brick spire, the elms,
　　　a green pond made out of
tourmaline, a stand that
　　　sells fried dough and plantains, a road

unzipping the black hills, and
then beyond it a fire tower like
a hermit's hut, commanding the best
　　　long view of outlying
areas. Black speck, a
　　　sparrow hawk circles an acre

of rough field, where wet new calves
thumb their heads through well-worn grass. In
winter it will flood slick ice. But this
    morning see how the calves
unbuckle in the soft
    dirt and stand up, each leg shaking.

VIII

The Angel of the Resurrection

Is it light on the trees
that turns them to pale fire
or is it spring, come without
    warning to this town on

stilts, set so precariously
above the river? All night my
heart is an owl perched on
    a high branch, its feathers

ablaze, its question answered
by the face of the Angel
of the Resurrection, reflected
    in water as your hand

prints itself on my bones,
head bowed, mouth an O,
burning, drinking the river
    in order to breathe.

IX

I spent days writing you a letter,
but can't find it now, and in
these first minutes of the last day

of the year had trouble, even,
finding a pen. Take these, then,
a few scratched words instead—

a knock on the door, a wink
from the deep—for when from sleep
you raise your head, this year

will be the river's other shore,
its penciled wharves washed over.
And what we thought then will be our

cargo on the ferry we take forth, as
we leave behind what happened there,
between those disappearing lines.

III

Heirloom

"Take it," my grandmother said. "You
　　might as well have it now."
"No," I said, knowing what now meant.
　　But I took it anyway, when
I left, leaving a white space　　—
　　a window where the picture went.

I brought it home and hung it up:
　　my grandmother, young, reading
under some trees. Red dress and shoes,
　　the same rooster red used, for
effect, on a rooftop skirting
　　a broad, heavy sky of news-

paper gray, her wide book a pair
　　of white goose wings, shedding
light on her face. What is happening
　　in those pages? She doesn't
look up, there's no hint of the artist,
　　my grandfather, dampening

his brushes a few yards away,
　　about as far as I sit
from her now, although to me,
　　at this distance, she's a good
deal smaller—a painted figure
　　in a painting. A tree

is a waterspout, a peaked roof
　　is a bird, a frill of roses verges
on a lilac hedge. And the orangerie

in back—a fantasy? A hotel?
He's painted the frame the exact shade
of the sky, wet streaks of greeny-

gray, as though if he just pushed out
the margin far enough, the packed
clouds might hold off forever. But
when the storm starts, won't they pack
up, go in? Barbed lightning might hurl
tridents on the uncut

lawn; my grandfather would have
closed his easel, my grandmother
her book. Or did she read on, staying
in the rain until the last
words of the chapter, a phrase so
long, it unwinds here, a fraying

wire that holds up a second picture
painted by the same hand,
fluent, now, on a matching square
of bristol board. It's late in the day.
Across a green smear of fields
a river swells to an inlet where

two children, poles taut in their hands,
are fishing. The boy is my father,
the girl, my aunt. On the surface
of the water the painter has drawn
himself in as a shadow, but what
he sees, we see: the open field

suffused with sun, the runnels stoked
   with darkness, the boy's smoke-swirl
of hair; twilight, the day receding,
   the girl's red dress an old one
cut down, as if this was the story
   my grandmother is so endlessly reading.

The Blue Moths

Blue roses
   papered the room.
      Robin's egg,

Della Robbia,
   Wedgwood, flax,
      the blue

of Fra Angelico.
   None of these.
      Last night, I saw

it again, when
   flocks of blue
      moths flit

to the mallow,
   their wings a shock
      of the lost

word, the murmur
   of what she
      called it.

Another Snowman

Lacy eyelet, and dark patches
of snowmelt, and paper snowflakes—

sharp as the bottle green leaves of
the blackthorn hedge. Outside, alone,

beneath the frozen tulip tree's
long limbs, a child builds a snowman

out of drifts. But what will he eat?
What will he wear? A hickory

stick. A hat, brand-new. "Who are you?"
asks the child. "I am the cold," he

says, "that you let live." She does his
charcoal buttons, snug and tight. Snow

falls. The afternoon spins. "What time
has wrought," the dream says, "I let in."

Lasting is hard. Too hard at last.
In love she holds the snowman's hand.

Valentine

The table's strewn. Scissors,
glue. Rice paper dyed lurid hues
sprouts heartfelt paddies
on scrubbed maple leaves.
Ventricle, oracle; a serpentine
love that speaks: across
a heart-shaped cake, a paper
girl, her pleated breast
a valentine, slogs through storms
of icing sugar, her snowshoes
leaving tear-shaped lakes.

Sleeping Child

Skiff, all night you spin.
In one league, your brow points
east, then your face moon silver,
you drift west. Less tranquil,
north and south hedge you in.
Not longer than the crib is wide,
you berth at every latitude,
brown bear at your foot, birds
by your head, and along your length
beasts congregate: dolphin,
seal, man-manatee; kin
in the blood-heat sea
that buoys you up.

Spell

Black wick, singed, that means to burn,
    drowning water, where the dry-eyed sun
drags its gaze along disastrous stones,
    fish bone, cold ground, malevolent leaf,
our gravity that leads us all to grief,
    to you, who watched me write this down:
while I am on this earth, and then after—
    where she will be, let breath be found.

Round for a Plague Year

In time remote from this new time
in brightness underneath the trees,
you laugh and cast your shadow down
in petals falling thick and fast.

Around a name we make a rhyme.
White bone and dust, blossom and ash—
we make as we will to the last
our shadows rhyme with dust and dance.

In time remote from this new time,
in dry grass underneath the trees,
a darning needle's silver flash—
spindle, plague, blossom, dance:

a blackened shadow hurrying past,
in burnt leaves falling thick and fast.
Waving now, you clap your hands,
bright petal turned to dust and ash.

Michael's Boat

When at night you woke
I sang to you, light in my arms
and your cheek wet, and the shore
    we rowed toward was sleep.

    Two a.m., four a.m.,
the sky brightening, our passage
abandoned as the last star
    to steer by faded. Milk

    and honey, trumpet vine,
the hours swelling in the thick
June heat as I crossed the wide
    floorboards, singing

    the only song that
settled you, as if you knew
even then the journey we were on,
    that we were leaving, or

    that I was, and you
would be forever heading into
open water, past gray shallows
    where the wrecked ship

    molts, splintering
at the high-water line, turning
from boat to felled kite:
    a beast whose rigging

should have let it
fly, but which withered instead
like the willow judged by
   Michael, "Let the Lord

   rebuke you." Shadow.
Inland. Four, five, six summers
pass. Too heavy now to carry
   when you stir, you rise

   instead, and walk,
somnambulist, around the room.
I sit up late. Asleep, you
   seem to know your way.

   Porpoise who swims
in the watercourse we made, I stand
on grief's upper deck and hear
   you ask, in the silence

   of the song's long
shade, "Whose boat is it, anyway?"
"It is yours," I think, but
   do not answer.

Psalm

(*Levavi oculus*)

Moon moss, goldfinch in the lavender;
baptisia, indigo's pretender,
    jetsam, driftwood, the sea's provender.

Bees snarled in the sweet peas, untended;
low the swing song the swallow suspended,
    locusts the hurricane upended.

Far knock of ship's bells, a horn bleating
across the long water's green pleating,
    the tide's endless parting and meeting.

And in the salt ditch between fir seedlings,
dragonflies, the quick whir as speeding
    they fly to the cattails, kneading

their lances, grass turning to tinder
    in June's flaring gentian, day ended;
the sky shot full of flight, repeating:
    Not the sun, nor moon by night, pleading.

Baby's Breath

No one could have expected it—least
of all me—what plant in the garden
   would run the longest

taproot. "I'll just be a minute,"
I said, and stood the shovel in
   the ground, standing on it

like a stepladder, in the maple's
surge of new-painted leaves. I stove
   and dug. I left off the shovel

and with my hands began to pry
the thing up from the dirt. Five
   fingers clutched me back. Dry

scrapings gripped the ivy. And then
I remembered its name, *Gypsophila*,
   and thought of the children

grabbing my sleeve on the Ponte Sisto,
their gay rags like the regalia
   of leaves now dropped into

the garden, grasping and pulling
until I felt we would all fall
   together, drowned, mewling

into the Tiber, back through silt,
through bitumen, to the heart's burial
   in the earth, our milk

white breath rising like clouds or
stars in the cold Roman air—
   like clouds, or like flowers.

Custody

A telephone rings in the vast house.
No shadow to the far-off sound,
but here dark gathers in high clouds,
as if the earth had spun around,
and through a telescope I see
the moon's cold cheek beset by storms,
black sky that cannot, will not pass,
carbon in sunlight's marigold.

My child is gone too far from me.
She is too fair, too wise, too old.
With every greeting she departs,
she goes to where I cannot go.
I know it, though—the logs are lit,
the beach fills up with party guests.
Ankle-deep, she stands in surf,
sand holding her as I cannot.

It's better than it could have been,
by far, since what once was turned out
to be some other way, and all
is well except it never ends.
Waves hug the shore with their long shrug—
the riptide that was out is in.
She moves to speak, I tilt the lens.
Soon this view will grow cold too.

Water Lily

In the dream,
a dream because
I will it

so, the bed,
a swimming pool,
folds down from

the wall, and
floating there, you
breathe without

a breath of
air, a lily
in your green

bathing suit,
gone still under
streaming hair.

This time too
I'm shook awake.
Shoot, lithe nymph,

quick bream in
water, life hewn from
me, my once

dry daughter.

The Swimming Pool

In the warm months before the baby was born
   I took the other children to the swimming pool,
  four flights below the university gym, down
    a long burrow of cool stairs. They skipped
      steps, eager to slide into the water. I held
    fast to the bent arm of the railing, pausing,
  stopping to rest, testing the tread with
    the full horns of my heels. At the bottom,
we split up. I went with the girls through one
      door, and Jack, at seven, through another.
    After the damp purgatory of the locker room,
  we came out the doors to the other side.

The pool was the clear sky blue of heaven.
    Banners hung from the ceiling, green, brown,
  orange, and crimson, and from somewhere off
    in the big echoing space, like the trill
      of macaws, or monkeys, rock music rattled
    from a radio, which was propped on the arm
of a chair that held a student lifeguard.
    His bleached thatch of hair stood straight up.
His eyes were closed. The pool was empty.
    The still water shimmied like aluminum.
Hummingbirds in their bright suits, shrieking
  —it was the first summer they all could swim—

they dove straight in, leaving me to lower
    myself into the cold sting of the lane
  beside them, where my slow crawl pulled me up
    on the rungs of green water. I swam
      with one eye open, counting their heads as

they surfaced like otters, their hair stuck
to their skulls, then watched them dive down
where, weeks ago, they'd found a window
on the wall of the pool. Cyclops, it looked
          into a little room: metal table, dilapidated
          chair, a door shut to somewhere. Nothing
could keep them from it but the need for air.

Despite the heat, we usually had the place
          to ourselves, so the day the other
children came to swim, at first I couldn't
          tell their noise from the splash we made
          in the water. But when I did, I saw
the steel locker room doors opening and shutting.
Most of the children who came out had difficulty
          walking. Each child held the hand
of a grown-up who urged them toward the edge
          of the pool, a few protesting, *no, no, no,*
until, lurching and stumbling, they came near
enough for me to see that they were blind.

My children continued to play underwater.
          For a minute I kept swimming, the pool
crowded now, the azure flashing with bodies
          and shards of light. Then I stopped, and
                    dove across the lane to where they were busy
at the window, writing their names in bubbles
on the glass. Shimmer. Cool in the gloaming.
          The blind children paddled close by, once
or twice jostling the girls. Others, swimmers,
          darted like sleek seals to the far end,
          their feet fluttering, leaving waves full
of pearls in the turquoise skeins of water,

and as I watched I felt my skin shiver green
with the baby, who would turn out to be
Beatrice, and I put my hand over her, though
I knew she was impossible to shield, or to
save from the idea of shielding, and with
my heart I smote the living that came near.
Gooseflesh. With my arms I hoisted myself
out of the water. "It's time to go home,"
I called to the children. Certainly, they
protested, pointing at the big pool clock
with mad gesticulations, as if their wrinkled
fingers, whirring through webbed air,

were the minutes that, by right, they had left
to them. "Now," I said, and they climbed up
the metal ladders, trying their best not to step
on the hands of the blind children, who were
clutching its slick cutting blades
for safety, even as they were being urged to swim
way out into the rough spirals of water.
We picked up our towels, striped yellow and mango,
lime and aquamarine, the colors of jujubes,
and trudged back into the hot day, first through
the locker rooms and into our damp clothes,
then flight after flight up the long, steep steps,

the high-pitched sounds from the pool melting
below us, the children snapping at each other,
deep in their chronicle of complaint, until
at the top of the stairs they were talking
instead, about the underwater window,
the eldest pretending she hadn't seen it,
which drove the others wild, as she intended.

All except the baby, whom I carried with me
another month, through days of record heat,
        including that afternoon on the walk home
      under the molten shadows of the heavy trees—
blind fish in her fleeting pool of waters.

Auden in the Aquarium

It was a hot day in June.
Inside the aquarium it was so cool
after the bright light outside that
it seemed as if we were swimming up
the arteries of a cold broad-backed fish.

We took in the crabs, the sea urchins,
the jellyfish that shone like
Japanese lanterns, and as we looked
our reflections flitted past us
on the green grass, animated, lit,

as if this was the shade to which
they are always hoping to return,
the reason they only show themselves
on surfaces that mimic water.
At some of the tanks the lights

had been arranged so there were
no reflections—it was like looking
through a window with the sash
raised—and it was at one of these
I saw you, Wystan, your crepe-paper

face on a huge tautog, swimming alone
in a clutch of striped bass.
The bass kept opening and shutting
their mouths like sheep, or choristers
—though their singing was completely

inaudible—and along their sides
were dark inky lines, like the marks
of tire tracks. There was an eel
there too, below you, its body
an S, then an O, at home, at least

it seemed, in its permanently
unitarian element: air filtered, fire
tamped down. The aquarium was filled
with schoolchildren, whistling,
shoving, with tourists in their

tropical clothes, waiting, as we were,
for the ferry to Vineyard Haven.
We stood at the tank. The glass was cold.
A tent of light shone down. Your scales
were the color of old silver, of smoke.

Behind you on the wall were a few
artfully painted sea grasses,
a few rocks, a wave but no sign
of a boy, and a warning:
        DO NOT TAP ON GLASS
for you to read backwards, in Icelandic.

A *Thank You Note*

TO JAMES WAGMAN

The magnum of Veuve Clicquot
bought to toast the Big New Year
was left undrunk and put away

until your August birthday,
when in the life we weren't sure
would come (as if time might

stop just for us) you pottered
up and down the half-lit dune,
passing it among the crowd

while sticky babies tottered
underfoot, and the ruined sky
recorded the sun's rapid

plunge from view in pumpkin hues
the exact shade of the champagne
label. Then turned flamingo pink

as stardust, the bubbles flew.
Now, summer shed, the bottle
sits amid crumpled flotsam

on my desk. Aggrieved, it
wears a lampshade on its head,
a reveler who'd hoped the revel

wouldn't end, but settles for
(though doesn't get) a glimpse
of revelation in its stead.

Nevertheless, it lights things up,
including this (raised to you)
chipped coffee cup.

Five Landscape Plants That Can Make a Difference

(after an article by John W. Oliver
in the *New York Times*, October 21, 1990)

I. VARDER VALLEY BOXWOOD

Persistent, green
    this small plant could be a dark
    standard. It can be, and here
    is, used as a foreground. Broad-leafed,

a Balkan native, ultrahardy,
    it travels well, curled tight
    as a hedgehog in its nest of newspaper.

II. PAPERBARK MAPLE

What else to read in the train
    but a thriller? Outside, the view changes
    from fire to snow, to water and grass,
    but beauty can be observed in all seasons,
        narrow, upright, peeling off winter white
        to reveal striking cinnamon beneath.
        In spring, it carries a corsage of leafy
red flowers. Why not have it? Few
mature specimens are available, but to see
this maple is to understand its charms. It's
at home in a multitude of landscapes.

III. DWARF JUNIPER

Star-shaped pelt draped over boulders, resistant
to drought, the juniper outlined in diamanté
   in the valley of winter is a pair of
   gilt-edged slippers: Mother Nature, going out.
      Who's crawling between rocks and ravines
   in the nursery looking to find a lost ribbon,
      the next minute toppling a house of cards?
   It's *Nana procumbus*. A bright stone sets up
the lushness of this beveled green mound.

IV. INKBERRY

   has few peers. Effective as a screen, it
   withstands pruning, thus is best used as
   a medium-sized hedge: a ha-ha, defined in
   the Universal as "a boundary to a pleasure
      ground not seen until almost upon
      it, a sunk fence." Make an island
      planting of this holly. Not compact,
      it gets leggy. The berries produce ink,
         but nothing it leaves is lasting.

V. BROUWER'S BEAUTY ANDROMEDA

      Pink buds in the rockery,
   the white flowers on green racemes, almost
      perfect of its kind for those who like it,
   a low-lying garden's Monte Bianco. Here
      is a place for a picnic. We have paper, ink,
   books, you've returned full of maps and plans,

your route marked in the red of the rose's
new growth. This plant's a hybrid. When
in the sky her namesake rises, we'll
lie back and count her starry eyes.

Ode

Each day is a song, you're always
humming. Although I would like
to compare it to "King of Glory,"
or "Now the Day Is Over," it's

a hymn to nothing, to songs you
heard once and forgot. Even if
I type like seven monkeys, I won't
find out that tune. So I carry on

as I am, stooped over at the start
of a century, still trying to rhyme
cat and *mat,* as I've sat before
you for thirty years. Or, since

my type tends to repeat—someone
like you. First, my father's
Royal Portable; then a borrowed
Underwood, excitable, all caps.

Next Hermes, the messenger. Now
you. Friends, children, uncles,
cats, came and went. Only we
seem to be forever. And I regret

that I never have any news to tell
you. With everyone else, I joke,
make love, give advice. You're not
beguiled by any of it, drinking

least of all. You haven't forgiven
me for scalding you with coffee,
that day I leapt to answer the phone.
Of course I answered it! It's not

the telephone who for months on end
has given me the cold shoulder!
And you should mind your p's and q's,
because by now, nobody knows

what I see in you! It's true, however,
you've never turned your back. Clearly,
though, to you it's all the same,
a row of x's or a poem.

Poem for a Birthday

I give you my *H*eart
    the size of a fist
I give you an *A*pple
    red as the world
I give you a *P*orpoise
    for how high it leaps
I give you a *P*earl
    moon from the deep
I give you *Y*arrow
    starry sunray
I give you *B*eauty
    brazen and furled
I give you an *I*ris
    spare indigo,
I give you *R*ome
    not built in a day
I give you a *T*roika
    to come and go
I give you my *H*and
    a matter of course
I give you *D*esire
    the rainbow's end
I give you *A*stonishment's
    bountiful stores
I give you the *Y*ears
    right round the bend

A Sighting

Another anniversary of your death.
A few of us, by coincidence,
are at the skating rink again,

this time, to be sure,
with infants in tow.
From the side I watch you dip and glide,

dear wraith among the figure eights.

I want to call to you but know I can't.
The air is cold, I catch my breath.
The child I'm watching hugs the edge,

until you who are each death this decade brought,
swoop close to guide him toward the fray,
and then return to where it was you came from,

saving a place for us,
who will in turn save one for him.

Rocking the Carriage

For years we kept one in the hall
and rocked the baby there to sleep,
up and down the long dim corridor.
It was a job that someone had,
laundry half-folded, papers unread.
Somewhere there was always fog
or snow, or so the radio said.
Rocking went on right through the zones,
past reckonings and acts of God.
So little happened in the hall
—the odd leak, a warped door not shut—
that often, lulled, I couldn't tell,
the child I wanted so to sleep,
was it Jack, Beatrice, or Rose?
The carriage wheels had turned so long
they wore a track into the floor,
and some days as I stood and pushed,
the pictures on the painted walls
were windows, and the hall, a train,
and down the railroad ties we rode,
past sunsets, cows, past bicyclists,
past towns. I liked a neon sign
that advertised an old racetrack.
Bright red, the horse and rider moved.
A clock. A steeple. Another train
charged backwards with a hiss.
We stopped once, halting sharply, to
let others in: an aged aunt,
a friend, just dead. Sandwiches were fetched.
My friend took out a book to read,
but though I tried, I couldn't see

the spine. (She couldn't answer, so
I didn't ask.) When lunch was done,
a girl got up to say good-bye.
"Oh look," I said, "you're all grown up."
She wasn't hard to recognize.
Her face grew small until, a cloud,
it rose above a pinafore.
"See you," she said. Then one by one,
the rest got on and off, as if she,
being the eldest, had shown them how.

The train passed through a clear cold night.
Trees were met once, the moon many times.
Hills undulated out of sight
as if the dreaming earth had stirred,
or a giant tossed a blanket down.
Then the view changed. A stony place
stretched out as far as I could see,
the distance held by a green maze
whose branches met above my head.
"Ssh," I said. "The baby mustn't wake."
With one hand I reached up and touched
the emerald mat of prickly leaves,
no hedge now, but a loose tweed sleeve
which I clutched hard so not to fall.
My step made bigger to match hers,
I swayed as if I walked between
two railway cars about to part.

And with my other hand I rocked
the grizzling baby in the hall,
willing no noise to break the spell—
the downstairs bell, a caterwaul,
a crying child, a train whistle.

A Note About the Author

Cynthia Zarin was born in 1959 in New York City and educated at Harvard and Columbia. The recipient of fellowships from the National Endowment for the Arts and the Ingram Merrill Foundation, and a winner of the Peter I. B. Lavan Award, she is an artist-in-residence at the Cathedral of St. John the Divine in New York City. She writes essays and reviews for a wide range of magazines and journals, including *The New Yorker* and the *New York Times*. She has published two previous volumes of poetry, *Fire Lyric* and *The Swordfish Tooth*, as well as several books for children.

A Note on the Type

This book was set in a modern adaptation of a type designed by William Caslon (1692–1766). The Caslon face, an artistic, easily read type, has enjoyed more than two centuries of popularity in the United States. It is of interest to note that the first copies of the Declaration of Independence and the first paper currency distributed to the citizens of the newborn nation were printed in this typeface.

Composed by Creative Graphics, Allentown,
Pennsylvania
Printed and bound by Edwards Brothers,
Ann Arbor, Michigan
Designed by Anthea Lingeman